To the Sun, where helium is light.
For the Earth, where helium is heavy.

Dedicated to Ann, Robert, and Abigail

Thanks to Vecteezy.com for help with illustrations.
Thanks to Judge Alex for his suggestion for the title.
Thanks to my editor and wife, Ann. Finally,thanks
to my family for being my inspiration to take on
this project and my motivation to complete it.

L was an empty list.

```
In [1]: L = list()

In [2]: L
Out[2]: []
```

Having length zero, left L feeling lonely.
In fact, being empty, L evaluated to False.

```
In [3]: len(L)
Out[3]: 0

In [4]: if L:
   ...:     print("The author of this book can fly")
   ...: else:
   ...:     print("Alas, there is gravity on Earth")
   ...:
Alas, there is gravity on Earth
```

One day, L encountered a bool by the name of False. L was overjoyed to meet her boolean friend to whom she evaluated.

L decided to append her new friend, False.

```
In [5]: L.append(False)

In [6]: L
Out[6]: [False]
```

After appending False, L was no longer empty.

Curiously, she now evaluated to the bool True.

```
In [7]: if L:
   ...:     print("Infants can learn Python!")
   ...: else:
   ...:     print("Infants cannot learn Python")
   ...:
Infants can learn Python!
```

Now that L was no longer empty, she was equipped to non-trivially employ one of her methods.

She could count!

```
In [8]: L.count(False)
Out[8]: 1
```

I HAVE THE POWER!!!

L began to get bigger ideas.

She wanted to know all the glory she was capable of and called dir on herself.

```
In [9]: dir(L)[-9:]
Out[9]:
['append',
 'count'
 'extend'
 'index'
 'insert'
 'pop'
 'remove'
 'reverse'
 'sort']
```

L had already appended and counted, so the next item from her dir to try was **extend**.

Since L already appended her only friend, and she didn't know anyone else, the only one she could extend was herself.

```
In [10]: L.extend(L)

In [11]: L
Out[11]: [False, False]
```

L was now doubly glad because she now contained twin boolean friends False.

Having tinkered with some of her methods, L was now ready to come face to face with a couple of the big guns of programming: the mighty for and the mightier function.

```
In [12]: def FUNCTION():
    ...:     """A one up to HelloWorld"""
    ...:     for b in L:
    ...:         print("Python is Fun!")
    ...:

In [13]: FUNCTION()
Python is Fun!
Python is Fun!
```

7

L noticed her function didn't take any inputs.

Scoping out the situation, L realized that she herself was global and accordingly in the scope of the function. In fact, her function, FUNCTION, was in globals too.

```
In [14]: globals()["L"]
Out[14]: [False, False]

In [15]: "FUNCTION" in globals()
Out[15]: True
```

L learned a lot in a short time. She was starting to feel overwhelmed. She needed help!

Fortunately, she inherited a lengthy document string from her own class, list. She also remembered that she wrote herself a docstring for her very first function, FUNCTION.

```
In [16]: help(L)

In [17]: help(FUNCTION)
```

L began to get a little philosophical. She pondered some of the great questions, like who she was and where she existed.

Using the builtins, is and id, L discovered she was who she was. Moreover, she was located at a random location in memory.

```
In [18]: L is L
Out[18]: True

In [19]: id(L)
Out[19]: 4402293936
```

L understood that she really could be more than a memory address. To achieve portability, she needed to be serialized.

```
In [20]: import json

In [21]: L=json.dumps(L)

In [22]: L
Out[22]: '[false, false]'
```

L was really just a json formatted string. In fact, L could be reconstructed very easily.

```
In [23]: L=json.loads(L)

In [24]: L
Out[24]: [False, False]
```

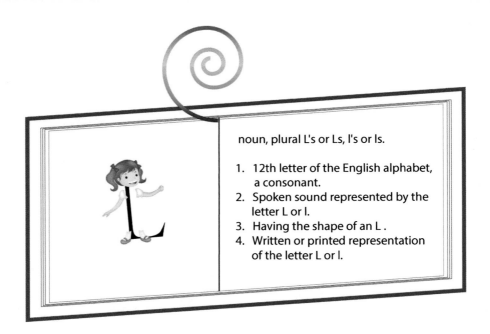

noun, plural L's or Ls, l's or ls.

1. 12th letter of the English alphabet, a consonant.
2. Spoken sound represented by the letter L or l.
3. Having the shape of an L .
4. Written or printed representation of the letter L or l.

Next, L ventured to explore strings and dictionaries.

To save time, she explored both at the same time. She reinvented herself as a dictionary with her entries as dictionary keys, and their strings as the corresponding values.

```
In [25]: L=dict({entry:str(entry) for entry in L})

In [26]: L
Out[26]: {False: 'False'}

In [27]: L.keys()
Out[27]: [False]

In [28]: L.values()
Out[28]: ['False']
```

I feel 11 pages younger!

Being a dictionary was a little confusing.
Fortunately, she could recast herself as a list.

```
In [29]: L=list(L)
```

Unfortunately, in the process of changing
back and forth, L now had length 1 again.

```
In [30]: L
Out[30]: [False]

In [31]: len(L)
Out[31]: 1
```

L noticed that a nice feature of containing one element is that it guarantees consistency.

Her **min** was equal to her **max**.

```
In [32]: min(L)==max(L)
Out[32]: True
```

Containing False was starting to depress L. Fortunately, with the help of the logical negation, she was able to turn things around.

Apparently, a double negative is good for something.

```
In [33]: L = not not L

In [34]: L
Out[34]: True
```

L really liked being the boolean True.

She was who she was, whether or not she was feeling like herself.

```
In [35]: L == L or not L
Out[35]: True
```

L was now the bool True.

But, through some quirkiness of typing, the result of herself plus herself was the number 2.

```
In  [36]:  L = L + L

In  [37]:  L
Out[37]:  2
```

Like any budding computer scientist who hits a wall of confusion, L was on the brink of calling quit().

```
In [38]: #quit() #commented out quit
```

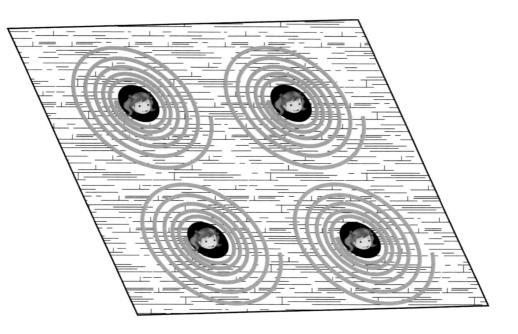

Trying to stay positive, L noticed that being a number did open up a whole new set of methods.

L decided to set herself equal to her range.

```
In [39]: L = range(L)

In [40]: L
Out[40]: [0, 1]
```

L could even **sort** herself.

Although, since she was already in order, **sorting** herself was trivial.

```
In [41]: L = sorted(L)

In [42]: L
Out[42]: [0, 1]
```

On the other hand, by employing the boolean True, she could reverse sort herself.

```
In [43]: L=sorted(L,reverse=True)

In [44]: L
Out[44]: [1, 0]
```

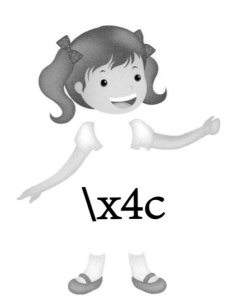

\x4c

L learned she could transcend the limitations of traditional character encodings by casting herself as a **unicode** string.

```
In [45]: L=unicode(L)

In [46]: L
Out[46]: u'[1, 0]'
```

But, she was more understandable as her old self. So she evaluated herself back to a list.

```
In [47]: L=eval(L)

In [48]: L
Out[48]: [1, 0]
```

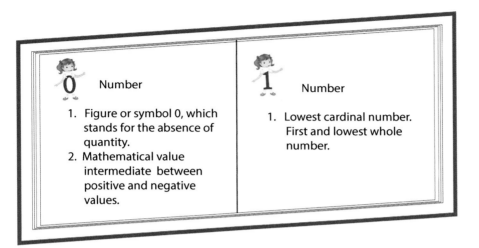

Now that L had two distinct members, she figured she could revisit her foray into dictionaries. This time, she wouldn't be shortened by the transformation.

```
In [49]: L=dict({entry:entry for entry in L})

In [50]: L.keys()
Out[50]: [0,1]

In [51]: L.values()
Out[51]: [0,1]
```

L had two keys and two values.

L had a long day and realized she was approaching the limit of her attention span.

She figured it would be responsible to at least post a **warning** sign.

```
In [52]: import warnings

In [53]: warnings.warn("Approaching attention limit!")
```

L looked back over her adventures. She had been a bool, a dict, an int, and a list. One thing she had not yet experienced was being an iterator.

Luckily, remembering how she turned herself into a range, L could be an iterator by just adding an x.

```
In [54]: L=xrange(not not L)

In [55]: L
Out[55]: xrange(1)
```

...well actually, an xrange is not technically an iterator. An xrange is an object which contains a xrangeiterator class extending the class iterator. An honest iterator ought to be constructed via a generator function including yields.

That said, given that L lives in a toddler world featuring tooth faries and Santa, we are probably okay calling an xrange an iterator. In any event, L rectified the situation with a one-liner.

```
In [56]: L=L.__iter__()

In [57]: L
Out[57]: <rangeiterator at 0x10c73a750>
```

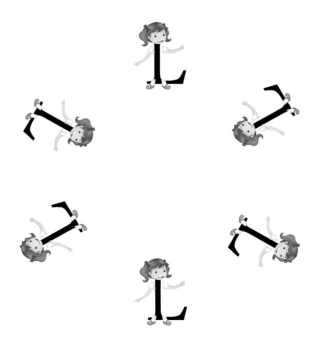

Being an iterator, L called next on herself and got zero.

```
In [58]: L.next()
Out[58]: 0
```

Because L was a one element iterator, L ended the day just as empty as she started. After all, though, it's not the destination, but the journey that counts.

```
In [59]: L=list(L)

In [60]: L
Out[60]: []
```

Made in the USA
Middletown, DE
10 September 2022

73463857R00018